A Single Mother's Journey

Ruth Brown

 www.trafford.com

North America & international
toll-free: 1 888 232 4444 (USA & Canada)
fax: 812 355 4082

Table of Contents

Acknowledgement

I appreciate everyone who has made this book possible.

Dedication

D edicated to all the Single mothers who do not allow their situation to deter them from being faithful to their responsibilities.

About The Author

Ruth Brown was born in the Caribbean. She shares her book of factual events - A SINGLE MOTHER'S JOURNEY.

This very interesting work outlines many of the struggles and accomplishments of single motherhood. It is very insightful and will definitely be beneficial literature to those who read it.

About The Editor

Beverly Grant is a born again Christian and was a property manager for many years.

Beverly enjoys writing and has successfully edited published works. She is currently working on her first book of poetry.

As an editor, Beverly has the ability to weave the author's "hidden spark" into the flow of the work; thereby capturing the reader's interest from start to finish. Due to her keen sense of attention to details, Beverly ensures that the sequence of events move the content along. This is her hallmark approach to editing. As a poet and songwriter, Beverly brings freshness and perspective to editing in a unique manner.

Introduction

Being a mother is not the easiest profession on earth. Being a single mother comes with even more responsibilities, decisions, and problems. Fortunately, it also comes with blessings. Mothers are not perfect: I am not perfect, neither was my mother, and children are certainly not perfect. We all make mistakes. We all do and say things that we sometimes regret.

There are no special instructions that come with mothering, because each case is unique. Each child is as different as night is from day and the prescription that is good for one, may cause illness in another. I believe that the first mother, Eve had problems with her sons Cain and Able. As a result, Cain committed the first murder, by killing his brother.

Those two boys had all the land and animals one could possibly own. They seemed to want for nothing, yet one brother was jealous of the other. The action of her son Cain must have caused grief to his mother. Eve was fortunate to have her husband, Adam to lean on. In the case of single mothers, they have no husbands.

Chapter 1

Single Mothers

There are different circumstances that cause women to become single parents. Some single mothers maybe divorced, abandoned by the father of their children, raped, widowed or their partner may be living in close proximity but is still distant. Some single mothers are adoptive parents. Although some people may look at single mothers with scorn, I have come to realize that being a single mother is not a crime.

Single mothers need to be embraced, especially if they are the sole care giver and provider. They should be honored because they have not abandoned or aborted their children. Life can sometimes be very challenging, especially for mothers who have no support for children who are disruptive.

Children who misbehave in public can cause onlookers to judge their mothers as being permissive, although they have no clue as to why the child or children are unruly. Although married mothers experience similar problems, it is more of a struggle for single mothers because they have no one to assist them. On the other hand, it is unfortunate that very few mothers receive compliments for their children's positive behavior.

I know from experience what it is like to retire at nights wondering about the next day; breakfast, lunch, dinner, school, work and all the details of each day. It does not take long for most single mothers to deplete their meager resources. It can be also agonizing to think of how the bank account can become empty a short while after the recent deposit was made. Some mothers get up very early in the morning to get the kids ready for school or daycare, after being awake most of the night trying to plan for the many tasks for the following day. Usually, after the kids are organized and off to daycare or school, the mother goes off to work, thinking about the chores yet to be performed. There is the laundry, the shopping, bills to be paid, going to see the teacher at school and preparing dinner.

Those mothers who attend church on Sundays, have to get everyone out of the house at a specific time for Sunday School and church service. Based on discussions I have had with parents, this process is usually a battle. The teenagers are aware of the time the family departs for church, yet they are rarely ready on time. The children know that it is mandatory in their home to attend church on Sundays, yet they protest. The head of the home, the mother has to be firm and has the final word.

Dr. Grace Ketterman states in her book, Mothering:

> "For many years our society has promoted a permissive attitude, lax disciplinary actions, and an emphasis on children's rights. There has been too little taught regarding children's respect for others and their sense of responsibilities. Children are more secure and exhibits the healthiest self-esteem when they know their limits."

If we refuse to set laws for our children, they will become lawless adults who will not be able to adopt to society at large.

Just as society has rules, the home should have rules. Everyone should comply or bear the consequences. When children fail to obey simple rules at home, then it will be difficult for them to obey teachers, administrators at school, leaders at church, and in adulthood, even supervisors. Since children receive their primary training at home, their first school, this training will help them cope in later years. It will prepare them to integrate into society. As adults they will not be surprised by laws, but instead will obey them.

Chapter 2

Single Mothers Speak

Hagar Laments

Well, ladies and gentlemen, my story commences this way. I am a very faithful servant of my master Abram and his wife. It is possible that no one will believe me, but I never had eyes for my master, Abram. This is the truth, the whole truth. I knew that my master Abram was my employer's husband, and all I desired to do was to be a devoted helper.

One night out of the blue, the unthinkable thing occurred. The only way I can explain it is that my master came in on me, uninvited. My story is found in Genesis Chapter 16. If you believe the Bible, then you know my story is true. My experience was a plan devised by Abram and his wife. Sarai was unable to conceive although she and her husband had tried for many years. Out of frustration she told her husband to know me in a manner that could impregnate me. So one night Abram came to my sleeping quarters and did exactly as he and his wife had planned. In modern terms, he sexually assaulted me, as defined by current laws. He molested me, a poor, innocent, helpless girl. There was no one to complain to and no court to defend me. I was very confused to see my boss come into my little room and use my body without my permission. I was aghast to see that so called important, outstanding community man, so close to me, in my very bosom. I know if this had occurred in 2018, Abram would be one of our public figures who would be in court, and possibly prison for violating me, and then abandoning my son and me.

Abram just did a 'slam dunk' and left me without any explanation. He showed me no form of affection. He left me, went to his wife and informed her that the mission was accomplished. I soon noticed that my monthly period had ceased, and my belly was getting bigger and harder to the touch. I began to have unusual feelings of discomfort in my stomach. Some days I felt really ill. Some of the meals that I used to enjoy made me sick to the stomach and I could not tolerate certain scents. One day I felt a kick inside of me and it continued intermittently. I had no one to talk to, I felt so burdened both psychologically and physically. At the end of nine months I gave birth to a baby boy, Ishmael.

In those days when a man had a boy child it was a special event, especially if he was the first son. I had given birth to Abram's first son and his wife Sarai was barren.

I began to mock Sarai. She became displeased with my behavior and complained to her husband. Abram told her to do as she desired with me. Sarai told Abram to send me away and he did. I was an innocent girl who became a single mother to a baby whom I had not planned for.

As we listen to the accounts of single mothers today, in the twenty-first century, we will have to agree with the writer Solomon, "History merely repeats itself. It has all been done before, nothing under the sun is really new." (Ecclesiastes 1:19 NLT).

Tamar's Peculiar Story

You may have to brace yourself for this series of events that is found in Genesis 38:6-30. A man by the name of Judah had three sons. The eldest Er, next Onan and last Shelah. Er married a woman named Tamar. Then God caused Er to die because he was wicked. In those days, it was the custom for the next surviving sibling to marry the widow of his brother and they should have children. Onan married Tamar and refused to deposit his seed during intercourse with Tamar. because he knew that the seed would be for his brother. Instead he spilled it. His action cost him his life because it displeased God.

Judah promised to give Shelah to Tamar when he was old enough. Judah was deceptive, he had no intension of giving Shelah to Tamar, because he thought Shelah would meet the same fate as his brothers. He was protecting Shelah. Judah told Tamar to go and reside with her parents. Tamar waited for Selah without success. She decided to set a snare for Judah, who had become a widower. She put on fancy attire and placed a veil over her face to disguise herself as a prostitute. She positioned herself at a strategic location where she could entice Judah. The plan worked perfectly. Judah went in unto Tamar and she conceived. She also caused Judah to give her several of his personal possessions. His identification seal, his bracelets and his walking stick. She planned to use these items as proof that he had been with her. It would appear that the pain of not getting Shelah as a husband caused Tamar to scheme against her father-in-law. Tamar being pregnant with twins is about to be a single mother.

Judah sent his friend with a young goat to give to the woman he thought was a harlot, and to retrieve his pledges. The friend was told by men in the area that there was no harlot in the area. He returned to Judah and gave him information that seemed most confusing.

Approximately three months later, the news reached Judah that Tamar was pregnant as a result of prostitution. Judah got so self-righteous that he took the law into his own hands and brought Tamar out to be executed; (burnt).

Does this not sound like the woman who was caught in adultery, but the man who made the adultery possible was nowhere to be found? Did she commit the act all by herself? Judah was so indignant that his daughter-in-law did not wait for his youngest son to become her husband, but instead became a harlot and was now with child. He placed the blame solely on Tamar.

Tamar was a woman who was not to be reckoned with. She was ready to be burnt. However, she brought out the pledges and explained that the owner of the items was the father of her children. She asked Judah if he had memory of them. Judah's conscience bothered him and he not only admitted that he was the father, but that he had wronged Tamar.

Tamar, this single woman gave birth to two boys, Pharez and Zarah. She is now inducted in "Single Mothers' Hall of Fame." Tamar, like thousands of other women, did not place an application for this special group of women, but she was inducted into it by her father-in-law. Shame on him.

The Widow of Zarephath

In 1 Kings chapter 17 we read an account of a widow of Zerephath. The name of this widow was not mentioned. God used His wonderful sense of humor, when He specifically informed the prophet Elijah that He was sending him to a village, to reside with a widow who would provide his needs. Prior to his commission from God, he was a fugitive who was fleeing from a wicked woman named Jezebel. Fortunately for Elijah, while he was in hiding, God sent a bird with dainty meat to him each day. God also provided a brook with refreshing water for him to drink.

As soon as Elijah entered the village, he saw the widow woman gathering sticks. He did not inquire of her about her welfare or her family; he immediately asked for a drink of water. As soon as the woman turned to fetch the water, Elijah made a second request for a bite of bread. (NLT).

The widow was probably wondering what manner of man Elijah was asking her for food. Certainly Elijah must have observed the situation prior to requesting bread from her. The fact that she was gathering sticks should have implied that she was of limited means. She also had a child with her, so it seemed obvious that she was responsible for the child. The child was not assisting with the gathering of sticks, perhaps because he was too young for the task. It does not appear that the widow had the child on a pedestal that would prevent her from assigning him chores.

In case you have never heard a single mother swear, this widow swore by the Lord, Elijah's God that she did not have a piece of bread. All she had was a handful of flour in a jar and a little cooking oil at the bottom of the jug. She was gathering the sticks to prepare the last meal for her son and herself, then they would die from starvation in the coming days.

After she explained her situation to Elijah, he did not seem concerned. He instructed her to bake him a little loaf of bread, before baking for her child and herself. He told her that if she complied she would subsequently have enough food for herself and her son until there was rain on the land. Her only provision was to be given to this stranger. She and her son were already facing imminent starvation. Although Elijah's promise seemed too good to be true, she reluctantly agreed to bake his loaf first.

Just as Elijah had told her, when she fed the man of God first, her house was supplied with food for the three of them. Elijah prayed a blessing on the home and whenever she went to the barrel or jug there was always sufficient to make them a meal. The food lasted until God sent rain and the crops were able to grow again.

A strange occurrence overtook the widow while Elijah was still staying at her home. Her son became ill and died. She blamed Elijah and questioned him, "O, man of God, what have you done to me? Have you come here to punish my sins by killing my son?" She blamed Elijah for her son's demise. She forgot her recent experience, how she thought her son would die of starvation and how Elijah caused God to resolve their problem by providing food for them. Her behavior must have caused Elijah some sadness. Elijah took the child from his mother's bosom and placed him on a bed.

The story took a different turn, because Elijah started questioning God about the tragedy. The widow had been kind enough to have him as a guest, and now her son was dead and she was blaming him. Elijah knew the God he served so he stretched himself on the child three times and cried to God beseeching Him to return the child's life. God answered Elijah's prayer and revived the child.

Elijah presented the child alive to his mother. This widow, a single mother stated, "Now I know for sure that you are a man of God, and that the Lord truly speaks through you." (NLT).

The Widow of Nain

There is a popular belief that states that children will live to bury their parents. However Luke chapter 7:11-17 gives a different view. This widow had no name. She was known as the widow of Nain.

The widow of Nain had buried her husband some time ago. This single mother and her only son were now living together. Tragedy struck again and this time her son died. Her son was her only help and now he was dead. She felt as if all hope was lost.

On the day of the funeral, the crowd of mourners and sympathizers gathered around the dead young man and his grieving mother. It is quite possible that the widow was worried about no longer having the required help for her living arrangement. As the procession began towards the cemetery, Jesus, the "Resurrection and the Life" was in the area. He saw the crowd, he saw the coffin baring the dead young man, and he saw his mother weeping. It is Hallelujah time when Jesus comes to town. He had compassion for the single mother and told her not to weep.

Jesus went and touched the coffin and the procession stopped. Then Jesus said, "Young man, I tell you: get up." (The message Bible). The young man got up at the command of Jesus. He began to speak and Jesus gave him to his mother. The crowd looked on in astonishment. They were amazed because they realized that Jesus was working miracles in their very presence.

They all acknowledged that they were in a place of holy mystery and that God was at work among them. They were quietly worshipful – and then noisily grateful, calling out among themselves, "God is back, looking to the needs of His people. (The Message Bible).

Comments From Mothers

Life of a Single Parent

I became a single parent at the age of nineteen. I thought it would have been "a piece of cake", but to my surprise it was far from that. Although I had well to do family members to help me share the load, the father of my child never helped in any way. His comment was quote, "This one is in good hands". Yes my family and I could afford to take care of my child, but the father also had a responsibility to help. To my surprise, he had three other children and one on the way.

At this point in my life I was so ashamed and humiliated because of my family background. I was brought up in a home where my family associated with upper members of society. I decided that I was going to migrate to a foreign country and try to make a better life for my child and myself. I wanted to redeem myself to my family. I was so fortunate that I managed to migrate when my child was four years old. I am still trying to make it up to everyone involved.

At the age of twenty seven I married a man with whom I was familiar, as an extended part of my family since I was 13 years old. I did not think he would hurt me, because he knew everything about my family from the outside to the inside. Little did I know that he was a "snake in the grass".

The marriage produced two children and this was the worst time of my life. My husband would not go to work he just wanted to gamble and drink liquor all day. Extra marital affairs was also a problem with him. My life was a living nightmare.

I pulled my boot straps up and did what I had to do to take care of my three children. I worked long and hard at the homes of various Jewish women. I took care of their children and cleaned their homes to get enough money to take care of my children financially. Believe me it was very rough sometimes, but through it all we made it.

In October of 1982 on a Sunday morning I went to a church service. The store front building was located behind a liquor store. My life was transformed from that day forward. The Pastor called me to the altar and told me some things that only the Almighty God of Heaven could have shown him. After he spoke to me I surrendered my life to Jesus Christ. Life began to look better for me. I continued to go to church with my children. I did better with my life.

I started to go to a community college after much encouragement from my friend. It took me ten years to fulfil my two year degree. I was placed on the Dean's List once and received an honorable mention once. Life has been up and down for me, but I believe there have been more ups than downs, thanks be to God.

During my struggles I managed to get a more prestigious job. I even bought a brand new car and a house, so that I could feel a little more secure in my life. I have learned how to lean and depend on Jesus. Because of His goodness and His tender mercies towards me, I too can say with God all things are possible.

I am now secure with my Jesus who has brought me along the way. I forgot to mention that I had dropped the dead weight from off me in 1983, when I divorced that infidel. Yes that infidel did not take care of his children. (1 Timothy 5:8).

I am free, my children are all grown up and my God is still taking care of me. I am healthy and still giving God the praise. So as you can see the single parenting life is not always hard. There are good times and bad times, just like anything else. I would not wish it on anyone, but when life throws you a lemon take it and make lemonade. God is always there with you and whenever you are too weak to walk He will carry you – I am a living example.

If you do not know Jesus as your personal Savior, today is the day to accept Him. He did it for me, so I know He can do it for you too, because He is no respecter of persons.

I hope my experience as a single parent will be a blessing to someone else and to all who will read this. I just want to let you know that with God all things are possible. Never give up because you do not know what tomorrow will bring you. Just accept Christ in your life, keep the faith and keep moving forward. To God be all the glory. I am a living breathing witness that God can do anything but fail. Glory to His name. Single parents, God is able to keep you from falling. Amen.

Making Decisions

Being entrusted with the gift of molding a life is always a blessing, however it is not an easy task. It is difficult to try and express the challenges one has to navigate through.

The financial aspect is important. There are times when I have to choose between getting something for myself and doing something for my child. As important as the financial decisions are, over time it gets derailed by the emotional, social and psychological needs of the child. I have to single-handedly make serious decisions regarding discipline and the actions to be taken when my child steps out of line.

We have had some tough times, but those times have given birth to strength and closer bonding. With all the hardships that we have been through, I am still grateful for the opportunity to observe my son's growth. I look forward with great anticipation, to see him fulfill his potential and be the man God created him to be.

Life as a Single Mother

No one plans to be a single mother. I never wanted to be a single mother, and had strong reasons. My mother was a single parent still living with her parents, under very restricting rules. Her parents were a bit disappointed in her, because she was in college when she got pregnant, and her dreams of becoming a teacher died. I had a lot of questions about my father, because I never knew him; but apparently everyone else did. I would walk along the street and hear that my brother was here or my sister was just ahead of me. Everyone knew him as the local success story and having many women. My mother answered my questions about my father, and I saw his reflection in the faces of the other children he fathered. I never wanted that for myself. I wanted a father for my children, who was first of all going to be my husband to give me a happy and perfect family.

Most little girls have dreams of a perfect wedding, with her father, (or grandfather, I inserted into my dreams) walking her down the aisle to give her away to her Prince Charming, who would be waiting at the altar. I was an avid reader, and according to the influence of the Mills & Boone Romance Novels, I would meet Mr. Right, fall in love, get married, have two boys and a girl, and live happily ever after.

Somehow, I messed up the perfect order of my life. I did meet Mr. Right, fell in love, got pregnant, got married, got miserable, and got divorced. So there I was a single mother raising a son. I promised myself to make my son's life better than mine. My son was not short of anything that he needed. I had a successful career, and could provide him with the material things he needed. We lived in a loving home with our extended family of grandparents, my sisters and cousins. Everyone helped to make sure he always had someone caring for him; particularly his doting aunts and cousins who provided the village I needed to raise him. He was happy, well loved, and had numerous friends, as our home was the one to which many of the neighborhood children, felt comfortable to visit, watch television or do their homework.

I never felt like a single mother because of the level of support that I had every day. I was not sitting home and bored because I had a full and busy life. Unlike me, my son knew his father. We had lived together as a family for the first three years of his life. After his father migrated and the divorce, my son still had the opportunity to visit with him and talk with him periodically before his death. My singleness was the absence of a husband, not the absence of a father for my child. When my sisters migrated and my grandparents died, I still had my sisters' love and support from afar, and the love and support from the people around me.

On reflection, I realize that the only time I was a single mother, was when I got married a second time. I was a wife and that took care of my singleness, but marriage did not provide an active father for my son. My son and I were not supported in a manner that we were accustomed to. There were no family members or friends around. There was no help I could call on. Technically, I was a single mother taking care of my son myself, providing for my son, supporting my son, being his emotional support and his disciplinarian. My days were consumed with working to take care of my son, and to provide for my son. For a brief portion of his teenage years, my son lacked both a mother figure and a father figure, until I got wise. I was a single mother only when I had the sole responsibility of rearing my child.

I would get home from work, and my son was not home. He would sometimes get home just ahead of me. He would be out without permission, and drive the neighbor's car without permission. Yes, I now have to admit that being a single mother was hard.

Living as a Single Mother

Living the single parent life is an experience which pushes one to a life of strength and weakness, happiness and sadness. We sometimes press towards seeing our children grow up fast and become responsible for themselves. However at some point while they are growing older, we miss that relationship with our dear sweet children.

I had a very busy life as a single mom and as a result I was constantly tired. I had to work at my regular job and work doing my daily chores at home. I always eagerly awaited Fridays, so that I could collect my pay, in order to feed my five children and provide for their other needs. I would anticipate the break of each day, so that I could fulfill the day's tasks. The nights seemed so long when sleeplessness stepped in and I forgot that God was my present help in my darkest moments. I pressed on slowly. I boldly executed the chores of preparing meals and doing the laundry, whether I was happy or sad. This continued day after day, after day, on and on as I was aging.

The memory of singleness is now like a dream since the children have grown up. I needed to spend more time with God. There were times when I did not know what to pray, although I had given my life to God. I knew that I should not have been afraid so I promised myself that I would pray every day.

My Single Mother's Story

I was attending teachers' college when I got pregnant with my son, at the age of 24. I believed his father would have married me, but he did not. Two years later after I started my teaching career, I got pregnant with my daughter. I had done the unthinkable, because teachers were not supposed to get pregnant unless they were married. You commit an 'awful sin' to bring a child out of wedlock. I was still hopeful that their father would marry me. He was a fireman and I was an elementary school teacher, so it seemed like we could enjoy a good family life together.

As time went by, I had no feelings for marriage, because the shameful time had passed. I had one intention and that was to migrate where I would have nothing to do with that man again. Being a teacher I decided to visit America for eight weeks at the end of the school year.

I had the responsibility of taking care of my children, so I hired the children's cousin, their father's niece, to care for them while I was away. That young woman took care of herself and her children, while she collected money from me for work she did not perform. When I landed in America I purchased clothes and sneakers and mailed to my home country for my kids. Although they were not in need, I could not resist purchasing those beautiful things for them. I thought of the children's wants and not my own.

I worked at my first job for a very short period. The lady of the house was eight months pregnant. She also had a baby whom she had adopted prior to getting pregnant. She left one evening to attend a birthing class while her husband was at home. I saw him reclining in another room. Since it was getting late, I used the opportunity to wash the kitchen floor. When his wife returned that night, he told her that he was prevented from having his dinner because I was washing the kitchen floor. I reported the incident to the agency and they gave me another job. My heart was broken when I saw the top floor that I had to occupy. Furthermore the furniture was terrible, the room left much to be desired and worse of all if I had to use the bathroom at nights, I had to go to the lower floor.

I made a legitimate complaint to the Lord, because I had left a nicely furnished, very clean and neat apartment where I lived previously. It felt awful to have to live in less than Third World conditions. You may not understand, but my little room in where I stayed on weekends was even worse, although I had to pay rent. On my first night in America, I slept on a little wooden bed with boards going across horizontally. When I got in the bed a piece of the wood fell off. I got up, picked it up and replaced it, then another piece fell off. This continued several times. It was not a peaceful, restful night.

This little closet of a room had a tiny closet, a little rough wooden table a chair and the bed. When I saw the bed in daylight the following morning, the mattress cover was dirty in capital letters and the pillow was messy. The bathroom that I had to share with a single man was filthy in every sense of the word. I went to the store with my sister-in-law and purchased cleaning supplies. I cleaned the bathtub and walls. It was not until after I was finished scrubbing that I saw that the tub was white. There was so much cobweb under the bed that I had to give the space a thorough cleaning. I washed the mattress cover and asked the landlord for money to buy paint for the room. The landlord told me that he would never purchase a new mattress for rooming house, but would pick them up off the streets. He was not a poor man, this I know because our relatives have ties to him by marriage.

The agency placed me in a new job to care for a young baby. As soon as I began working for the family, the mistress dismissed the cleaning woman and added her tasks to my job. Her husband told me that he had asked her not to dismiss the cleaner, but his request fell on deaf ears. I worked from six in the morning until late at night. I vacuumed so much, that I had a swelling under my armpit. When I worked as a teacher, I had a woman who cared for my home five days each week. She also cared for my babies until I got home from school. When the children were older, I employed a day's worker to take care of the house and the laundry. I was not unfair to my helpers.

I worked for several families. One of my employers sometimes acted like a crazy person. Not even her mother could visit for longer than a week. She treated me very badly. Some of her friends said that I knew something about her that they did not. There were times when she was ill and I cared for her, and as soon as she recuperated she abused me. I tried to be patient because her husband was planning to assist me to live more comfortably in the United States.

My Employer spent very little time with her baby, so he gravitated to me. One night when his father came home and saw me caring for his son he said, "No wonder he thinks you are his mother." On one occasion she told me that if I left the job, they would find the baby in the woods. She did not want a child but her husband did. The older the baby got, was the more he clung to me. He even gave me a special name.

After the child started pre-school one day I accompanied his mother to pick him up. When we got home she took him upstairs and I went to the kitchen to prepare his lunch. She called me and as I was ascending the stairs she came down and suddenly lifted her foot to kick me. She was a size six and I was a size sixteen. I went back to the kitchen to get the knife to continue preparing the lunch. The only knife my hand took out was a large butcher's knife. I immediately remembered my children and put the knife back in its place. I called one of my fellow teachers who was part of a support group for us while we were away from our families. We were all living and working in the same area. It was good to have someone to talk to. I had my children in mind and knew that if I got in trouble I would be deported and my children's future would be in jeopardy.

One day my employer was holding her son as I was giving him his medication. He started puking and she hurled the vomit at my face. She told her husband that she was flashing her hand and the vomit accidently got on my face.

It was a very cold fall day, and I cannot recall the reason for her anger, but she threw a cabbage at me. I walked out of the kitchen as she used a curse word and told me to leave her house. I went to the street, stopped a motorist and asked for a ride and a little change. I was happy that I knew the business telephone number for her husband so I called him. He instructed me to remain at the park until he got there. The train station was close to where the motorist had left me. Although I was cold I had to sit and wait for him. He came and took me back to the house.

I loved the child and cared for him for about three years. He would sometimes climb out of his crib very early in the morning, come downstairs and get in bed with me. I was afraid of his mother attacking me, so I would get out of bed only to hear him plead, "Don't get up". I made up my version of "Jesus loves me this I know," and included little the child's name, my son's and my daughter's names. I missed my children very much.

Some of the people I worked for gave me garbage to eat. In some instances, their dog got better chicken than I got. I refused to eat their unpalatable food, because I ate better food when I was back home. I started to buy meat and fish to take with me to the job. When I relocated to another area, I recall working for a woman who made me work extremely hard. My reward at dinner time was a piece of veil so small that it looked like a tiny map of a country. That Saturday night I placed it in the freezer so that I could take it to show my relatives. On Sunday morning the employer saw me opening the freezer and questioned me. I told her that I was taking the dinner she gave me last night home to show it to my relatives.

I resided in America for twelve years without seeing my children. Although they did not have my physical presence, telephone calls were made to them on a regular basis. I mailed packages, and the barrels with clothes, food and toys kept pouring in for them year after year.

Be assured of this, if I were not concerned about the welfare of my children, I would have done some things differently. My world revolved around my two children, because they had no one else to care for them. I prayed and asked God to take care of them. I committed them to Jesus.

I visited my doctor once and he detected a lump in my breast. He told me to contact a surgeon, who told me that even if I had cancer I would have to wait for a month for an appointment. All this time my mind was on my kids. I was not concerned about death, but my thoughts centered on my children. I wondered who would take care of my teenagers. My former church had Pastoral Prayer every Sunday morning, so I went to the altar for prayer that entire month. After lifting my faith I felt my breast and the lump had disappeared. I called the doctor and informed him that I was not going to see the surgeon because the lump was gone.

After so many struggles and a very difficult life, the Lord enabled me to visit my children and family members after twelve years. I filed an application for my children to obtain their Permanent Resident Cards. They arrived in America shortly after their applications were approved. We attended church together and they both gave their lives to the Lord. I sustained them until my son enlisted in the United States Army, where he served for twenty years. My daughter attended university in America and God has richly blessed her. She is now a physician.

Life as a single mother can be very challenging, but love covers it all.

Chapter 3

Instill Certain Morals

In Proverbs 22:6 we read "Train up a child in the way he should go, and when he is old he will not depart from it." (NKJV). We live in a society where the word morality seems to be a word of the past. Very soon our children will be asking us if that word is in the dictionary or if they can google it to find out what it means.

There was an account of a married couple having sex on a table outside a fast food restaurant. Patrons were observing, and this took place in view of the playground section of the building. The couple said that they felt like doing it there, and did not see themselves doing anything indecent. Sex is a wonderful thing that brings joy when it is done at the right place between married couples, but certainly not on a hard bench in the public.

Riders are allowed on the Subways wearing skimpy clothes below their waists at a certain time during the year. In some parts of the world, ladies who want to show their breasts just need to paint their upper bodies. That is all the covering that is required. In our society today, everyone can dress however they desire and they cannot be denied that right.

Every family has a different expectation, but we must steer our children in the right path. I remember a remark made by a wise man. He said "Anything that is advertised too much is not good." It is refreshing to know that some of us respect our bodies and refuse to expose our private areas to the public. Contrary to popular belief, there are people who have certain morals they learned when they were growing up. It was the norm in earlier years to behave in a respectful way and dress modestly. Many people from that generation have not outgrown or abandoned those ways. Properly attired people do not feel pressured or old fashioned when they act like decent citizens.

There are times when the media seems to encourage society to act immorally. Sometimes when we view some of the movies, commercials or soap operas on television there is little left to the imagination. From time to time, children are left unsupervised to watch the wrong cartoons and programs that give them an incorrect message.

There are hardly any role models for our children to emulate. Our young people listen to rap songs that contain filthy suggestions and words. The lyrics have nothing uplifting for our youngsters but that is what some of them like to hear. In fact, they enjoy that type of music. It is sad to hear these noises emanating from the airways and to witness their popularity; it is likely seductive. We have to instruct our children at an early age to embrace the positive things instead of the negative. Some of our children may stray from the right path, but they have a conscience that will always remind them of how things should be.

I read on a bumper sticker, "An unleashed dog is an Unloved Dog." I am not suggesting that our children are like dogs, but instead I am saying to some people their dogs are like kids to them. They sleep in their owner's bed, sit on their laps and interact with the family. They even have the family name. All I am saying is, if we love our children we will train them and point them in the right direction, just like we do with our pets.

I recall the family devotions that I had with my children. My children were very young and we would pray together. A co-worker (an elderly woman) suggested that I have devotions with them. I was happy for the suggestion and complied. I called on them to pray individually and they responded in their own simple way, but their prayers were earnest. When they began attending private school, we sang Christian songs from their School Song Book. I had hopes that this would have lasted all during their growing years, but things changed. After they migrated to the United States and joined me, we continued devotions for a while, however because of our daily schedules we had to discontinue. As head of the family, I take the blame with valid excuses. Being the sole bread winner, the person doing the errands, and paying the bills, trying to cope was somewhat overwhelming.

I take the liberty to remind some of us and inform others that the best or most effective method of training children is by setting an example. Children will observe us and want to be like us. Have you heard of a little boy who tried to imitate his dad by trying to shave his face? Our children will not always do as we do, but let us be the best role models for them. "Habits are more easily caught than taught", so if we do not want our children to smoke, we should not smoke. If we don't want them to cheat, when we receive too much change after making a purchase, we should return the excess. We do not want them to tell lies, so we do not promise to be home at six o'clock and arrive at six-thirty without an explanation or a call to say we are sorry, but we will be a little late. Parents who do not want their children to drink alcohol should not drink alcohol or have liquor in the home. The days when we used to hear "Do as I say but not as I do," are long past. Children are more combative these days, and will confront us with these truths.

When we give an ultimatum, we should be certain that it is one that can be implemented, and be sure to follow through with it. If you inform your child that if he or she comes home after everyone has eaten dinner, a privilege will be revoked, unless there is a legitimate reason for being late; then you must revoke the privilege if your instruction is defied instruction. Do not go back on what you have said, that action will only guarantee that our children will not respect our authority.

Many parents do not like when children remind them that they are unfair. I recall stories of creditors calling on the telephone and the parent would tell the child to say they were not home. The innocent child would tell the creditor "She says she is not home."

Chapter 4

Teenage Mothers – Single Mothers

Teenage mothers are merely children themselves, having babies they are unable to care for. They are unprepared physically, mentally, educationally, spiritually, socially, financially and emotionally. Some teenagers have made an effort to be good mothers under very extreme circumstances and with little or no supervision and parental assistance. Many of these teens have not completed high school, and after having one child they sometimes have one or two more. Their chance of getting a proper education or a well-paying job slips away. We have to encourage our children to abstain from sex until the appropriate time.

I am not an advocate for abortion. Some women may have one chance to become pregnant and if they should have an abortion, then they will never be able to conceive again. Abortion is a sin that leaves ugly scars, especially emotional ones. An abortion is not the answer for an unplanned pregnancy. If someone has had an abortion, I will not be the judge, and I can introduce that individual to someone who forgives sins, and that includes abortion.

If the pro-lifers or the church community wants to discourage abortions, they should establish crisis centers where pregnant teenagers and young mothers who do not want to keep their babies can have material, physical, spiritual and emotional support. If these mothers had a place of refuge, and caring people to assist them, I think many of them would accept that alternative. Currently, some schools provide nurseries so that mothers can have their babies cared for while they are in school.

There are alternatives to abortion and adoption is one of them. These unwanted babies can be placed with a good caring family who wants a child. This option is much more acceptable than taking the life of an innocent child, even at one day of conception. If someone becomes pregnant because of poor planning she can use the unfortunate situation to bless a family who longs for a child.

Children are not prepared to rear children. I think some of these young girls see babies on the television cooing and smiling and they mistakenly think that is all there is to parenting. They do not understand that they will never get a break, and that parenting is not something that they can stop doing because they no longer feel like it. I do not encourage young children to do babysitting at church or at home, because they may simply conclude that since they are capable of caring for a child they are ready to get their own as soon as possible. It might not be verbalized but the thought and action are sometimes obvious.

The television programs rarely display a baby who is crying uncontrollably, especially at nights. It is very frustrating for the single mother who is usually up all day and is alone at night with a sick or fussy child. Some mothers just cannot cope. I can recall my son (my first child) at about two months old crying for almost a week. He started every day at approximately 1:00 p.m. and ended about 7:00 p.m. . I was twenty four years old and it was a stressful time with no grandparents close by. I tried to breast feed my son and he cried. I walked around in the room with him in my arms and he cried. He stopped crying only when he took short naps and feedings, but still the crying seemed endless. As difficult as the situation was, I was patient with my baby and never abused him. After that segment of crying, my son was the best baby in the world. He became a little social being with all the qualities that one would expect from an angel-child. As an adult he is still a quiet social being. My daughter was born two years later and it was quite different. She did not have a crying spell. In fact no one could tell that there was a baby in the house because she was so quiet. At about two years she would cry if anyone came close to me. She was very attached to me and was very jealous of me. She did not want anyone near her mom.

Although my daughter was a toddler, I tried to teach her not to disrupt me when I was having a conversation with someone. She interrupted anyway. It was easier for me to say yes or no to her than to say "I am talking." She was usually satisfied with the short answer I gave her. As soon as she awoke in the mornings she began calling her mommy and never stopped until she found me. One morning I was at the back of the house and did not know what was happening. As soon as I got in close proximity to her and my landlady my daughter said "you lied, you said that mama was not here." I was perturbed because I did not expect my young child to react in that manner to an adult. I started to scold her but she continued. The landlady then said that she had told her I was in the back. My daughter insisted, "No, you said mommy is not here." I was not sure of what to say or do. I did nothing because I knew that my baby was speaking the truth.

Single mothers like teenage mothers are left with the responsibilities of making the home for the family and providing in every sense of the word: the discipline, babysitting, medical decisions and all other tasks. Some mothers do not discipline their kids and others do so in an abusive manner, taking out their frustration on the kids. Some women remain single by choice while singleness is thrust upon others for a variety of reasons. Many children without fathers are living in poverty. Some of the fathers relocate and start a new family, while deserting their first children. There is a case where a young man travelled very far to find his father, who treated him very unkindly. His father asked his new wife to call the police and told his son that he never wanted to see him again. The young man explained that he did not want anything from him, but he just needed a relationship with his father. The son was so ashamed he went to his car and cried.

Mothers are sometimes unaware of the scars our children have because their fathers have abandoned them. When we observe children acting in disobedience or in a disrespectful manner, they may be blaming themselves for the absence of their father. Some children abuse their mothers and those children should be put in a place where they would be punished for their unacceptable behavior. There is no reason for a child to physically or otherwise abuse his mother and siblings. It could easily be assumed that an abusive child will ultimately abuse his or her spouse. We should therefore try to stop it so that it does not continue in an endless cycle. The conflict with children is not unique to any one group or culture, but spans the entire society. I attended an In Service Training on, "How to Live with a Teenager and Keep your Sanity." A single mom shared that whenever a male relative visits her home, her child exhibits proper behavior. This gives credence to the fact that a male presence in her home contributes to discipline.

There are schools for chefs, tractor trailer drivers, nurses, bank tellers; tapes on how to repair appliances, how to stay physically fit and the list continues. Unfortunately there is no school for mothering. In making a pizza, you put the crust followed by the filling of your choice, but children are not like that; they are intricately created. Psalm 139:3-16 tells us how a Divine Creator made us. "My substance was not hid from Thee, when I was made in secret, and curiously wrought in the lowest parts of the earth." (KJV 139:15). It is difficult for a mother to experiment with a formula that is presented to her to use for raising her child. It is hardly likely that it will work. There are people who do not mean any harm, but they have never had children to contend with. They try to give prescriptions on how to care for kids and although their intentions are good, they would need to trade places with us mothers for a year or two. I recall a set of fraternal twin boys who looked and acted very differently from each other. One would isolate himself from his parents and me, while the other was close to us. There were times when we would be asking for the smaller of the twins, while he was safely entertaining himself.

It is challenging being a single parent for several reasons, but we have to remember that we were the ones who gave birth to these children. They did not choose their families, they were simply born into a family, and no matter what happens it will still remain their family.

As single mothers our task is great. Raising children alone is a long tedious journey, but if we trust God (my Lord, King and Savior, Jesus) He will place things in its proper perspective. God is depending on us to train our children (especially by example) in the right way and to do our best for them. We might not be rewarded with earthly goods, but we will hear "Well done." The reward may take years to come, but it will definitely come.

Chapter 5

Crime and Violence

These days crime and violence are taking place in the home, at the workplace, in the schools, on the streets, in shopping areas and even in some churches. Each and every day the newspapers are filled with sad stories of crimes that have been committed. The television, internet and radio are always reporting some violent act about someone who has become a victim of some sort of crime. There does not seem to be much good news these days. It almost seems as if reporters conceal the positive stories and publish the negative ones. One does not turn the news on without hearing of a heartbreaking report about an infant, a child, a male, female or an elderly person who has been victimized, abused or killed.

I think family members should inform the family as to where they are going, and if possible what time they will return. I realize that it may be difficult for a young man of nineteen or twenty years to inform his mother that he is going to the store and will return shortly, but it is prudent for him to explain his plans to her. If a family member is away from home and there is a newsbreak, invariably the first question that crosses the mind of the parent is; what if something has happened to my child? When we love our family we will have their best interests at heart. Innocent citizens are sometimes caught in drive-by shootings and crossfire and are killed because they are at the right place at the wrong time. It has become customary to locate bodies at different areas on the street. We are not at war and yet, our soldiers who are private citizens are gunned down daily.

One sometimes escapes the gun, but someone drunk or otherwise impaired might drive an automobile into pedestrians, killing them. Private citizens and law enforcement officers are murdered and it seems as if there is no end in sight for this problem. Animals seem to have more rights than people, because Animal Rights Activists are always protecting the killing of some animal or other. Even rodents have rights and their day in court. Children are being killed on the streets and in the home by children themselves.

Year after year I have observed young men in caskets being taken to the cemetery before they celebrate their twenty-fifth birthday. When my son was young I did not want him to become a statistic. I wanted him to grow up, have a profession and a family of his own. Regardless of his objectives, I refused to see him standing at a corner on the street or in front of a store without a valid reason. If he had to wait for the bus, then that was a good reason. If it hurt his ego when I told him that the street had an ominous cloud over it and that is not where he should be, then he would just have to become upset. I would not like to have to go to the morgue or hospital to identify my child. Loving your kids often means that you have to administer tough love. I have seen many mothers, single and married weep for their sons and all sorrow is similar. Those of us who know how to pray must pray for all children, because there is an attack from Satan on their lives.

Violence in the schools makes learning almost impossible. Under such circumstances, it is difficult for teachers to teach. With children fighting, throwing things around, making noise and in a state of lawlessness, it is unreasonable to expect teachers to teach in such chaos. Some children are afraid of their peers because two or more of them bully one that is decent and helpless. Some teachers are afraid of the lawless children as well. Some children even threaten their educators, and some parents have the nerve to blame these teachers if their children do not graduate. It is a shame to have children staying home, away from an education because of fear. Many children have committed suicide because of their fear of bullies. As mothers, let us make an effort to instruct our children in the right way. The right way is to read the Bible and pray that God will rule in the lives of our kids. In an affluent country such as America, children should not graduate from high school unable to read, while people who reside in poverty in other areas are literate.

Violent crimes of all sort take place in the homes of the rich as well as the homes of the poor. Children, women and young men are abused and killed in the home as if they were on a battlefield. People who once professed their love for each other are now eradicating the ones who trust and love them. May the Lord help us at home, school and in the streets. Sometimes the violence is not publicized by family members until a crime such as murder, which cannot be concealed is reported or discovered. Very often family members are too frightened or embarrassed to seek assistance when there is a problem in the home. They just refuse to give anyone a glimpse of the wrong that is taking place. Seniors hide abuses, children hide abuses, wives and sometimes even husbands hide as well. If one is unsafe in his home, there is hardly anywhere else where he will be safe.

Sexual abuse in the home is common and has been for a long time, but no one wants to disclose it. The victims are usually afraid that if someone is aware of it, they will be ostracized and victimized again. Some victims cannot reveal such matters because of threats of being killed and because of possible unbelief from a parent, who should be the one to protect the victim, (her child). It is difficult to think or believe that a father, step-father, brother, mother or other family members would dare to perform sexual acts on their innocent relatives, but it happens all too often. Men are not the only ones guilty of these abuses, because mothers also abuse their sons and daughters. Victims should report these crimes and seek counselling, so that they can be assured that they are not responsible for what happened to them.

We confess that we are a Christian country, but what do we really mean by that statement? For so many, it is only when crisis strikes at our door then we remember God. We sometimes wear Christianity like a garment we can put on and take off at will.

I want to share two narratives where people could have been violent but changed their minds. My parents told me about a man who went to a school to accost the male principal because he had spanked his son. When the father arrived at the school, the principal took his strap to him. He became so scared that he immediately started running. The principal chased him but was unable to catch him. That was many years ago. What I am about to relate happened when I was a teenager. One day two Pre-K girls had a fight. The older sister of one of the girls got involved. She was dissatisfied with the outcome of the fight so she went and got her mother, the neighborhood bully. The principal intervened and questioned the older girl as to why she got involved in the dispute between the girls. The principal told the sister that she deserved to be spanked for interfering, and getting her mother involved. She spoke in a voice so harsh that it sounded like a bark. She then turned to the mother with that harsh voice and asked her purpose for coming, (this was a kind, loving principal, but she was very authoritative). The principal then told the mother to get out. The mother who had come with such arrogance, walked out like a lamb. Society is different now and it is rather sad; people walk in fear because of other people.

Chapter 6

Achieving Goals

Everyone should have a goal in mind. The athlete runs because he or she expects to finish the race and win the prize. Before he or she enters the competition extensive practice and conditioning of body and mind is paramount. The athlete has to have the proper diet, get adequate sleep and rest and eliminate alcohol from his or her diet. All this preparation is necessary to enable a competitor to effectively compete in an important event. It is difficult for a serious athlete to go through this grueling process alone, therefore a competent coach is necessary to give guidance and instruction when necessary. All mothers want to see their children work towards their goals. Single mothers sometimes need a coach to help her along and assist her children. We can reach out to our friends, our pastor or a guidance counselor for assistance.

I am convinced that children from single parent families, especially with mothers as the head of the family, can become outstanding members of our communities. There are prominent leaders of our country, who had no father at home, but mother was there to fill the gap that father left.

I see little difference between a child from a single parent home and a child with both parents attending the same school. Yes, emotionally there may be some difference, but these children have the same opportunity to learn. There are homes where the father is present in body but he does not contribute materially or financially to the child's needs. He does not communicate or play with his child. There is absolutely no interaction. He might be there because society will make negative remarks about him if he leaves. He is either sleeping, watching the television, reading the newspaper, on the internet or even working. In any case he is unavailable.

Children in a one-parent family home have the potential to become presidents, priests, police officers and postal workers, just like other children. They have to set their goals, work towards it and achieve it. I have never seen a sign or heard of a case where children were segregated because they were from a family with their mother as the head of the family.

All of these children are given the same opportunity. They might lack the finances but they have similar equal rights. I grew up with both of my parents. I had goals, worked towards them and achieved them. Although my children grew up in a single parent home, they were no less determined to be the best that they can be. I pray that parents will encourage their children to remain in school. Parents must make an effort to help kids to scan their horizon and achieve their anticipated goals.

Chapter 7

Parent Support Group

In past years, there was a strong male attendance at church services. It is a sad reality, but there has been a decline in male attendance, thus our boys and girls have fewer role models. There is no father figure in the majority of homes, so there is hardly anyone for our boys and girls to admire and respect. There are "Big Brothers" groups, but not all churches have access to these groups. There are camps for boys, but we hear of horror stories regarding some of the counselors. In some situations, by the time it is discovered that a boy has been violated, it is too late to respond in a meaningful way. The action just cannot be reversed.

There is an urgent need for Christian parent support groups in our churches. A mother might be uncomfortable informing a pastor or church leader about her concerns, but will discuss the challenges she is facing with her peers who are experiencing a similar situation. Mothers and fathers would be able to share ideas on how to solve certain problems that they are encountering. Some families are hurting and are afraid to disclose their deep hidden secrets. They might confide in friends, but friends usually have limited capabilities to respond appropriately. Parents in support groups will be able to cry, share and pray together. They will have trust in the group, knowing that whatever they discuss will be held in confidence.

Group discussions can be effective and it is less expensive than going to a therapist. All parents single or otherwise, can benefit from a caring group of people who are willing to listen. We all like to have someone who listens without interrupting. Someone who will not blame us for the hurt we are feeling, but instead will empathize with us.

Many years ago a minister suggested that male adult members of the church "adopt" a boy whose father did not reside in his home. This person was to develop a relationship with the child, gain his confidence, do activities with him, inquire about his school work and talk with him. Unfortunately, we are now living in times when we are apprehensive about leaving our sons in a one on one relationship with a man. We simply do not know who to trust with our children. I am not judging men, especially those who are affiliated with the church. I am just stating the fact that we do not know when or who to trust, so the safest way is to be careful.

Our sons need role models in order to pattern their lives. Thank God there are still some men around us who fit into that category. Our sons can learn how to prepare a meal, clean the house or to do any of the thousand and one chores a mother does. Their assistance does not have to be limited to the aforementioned, but it would be a start. Some men in church have a wealth of information to offer our boys. When our boys observe how these fathers care for their families, their participation in church and community activities, they will have a sense of how to behave when they are older. Some of us think we would like our husband to be just like the pastor, because of the good qualities he displays. We see kindness in his family and listen to the tenderness in his voice, even when he is being stern. Our sons need big brothers who will teach them acceptable behavior, even without uttering a word – just by their examples. An "alternate lifestyle" is not for our sons. We want them to get married to the opposite sex and produce sons and daughters.

I doubt that any motorist would like to start his car and find that it sounds like a Harley Davidson motor cycle, or a helicopter. Likewise, we do not want our sons to be anything other than a man. No mother wants her son to be portraying attributes of a woman, with the exception of love, compassion, cooperation, gentleness, faithfulness, working hard and kindness. Men should be excellent providers, strong and wonderful lovers. Above all he should be a man on whom God can depend. We expect our sons to look like men, act like men and be men. God is relying on men for procreation of the human race. Boys, your future wives are depending on you to support them and your children.

Chapter 8

Conclusion

Single mothers, God knows the hurt that you have felt and are feeling. Remember that He cares for you and will not leave you alone. In the past I thought of ending my life but God sent help, and He has been my constant source of strength. There were times when I thought that I would run away from home, but I did not have anywhere to go. It might seem strange to hear that the head of the household wanted to abandon the ship, but problems can cause us to feel that way. When you feel overwhelmed, just remember, "For God hath not given us a spirit of fear, but of power, and of love and of a sound mind." (2 Timothy 1:7). When you have done all that is humanly possible and things and situations do not improve, continue to pray and wait for God to act.

As mothers, we have pledged to remain actively in our children's lives until they are on their own. If after they have left home they have a valid reason to return for guidance and assistance, we have to try and help them to the best of our ability. We were there when our babies laughed, cried, called, required changing; when they were hungry, when they needed their baths, when they were ill, when they fell and got up again and when they just wanted to be reminded of our presence. We love our children more than words can express.

Let us pray for our children and there will be less pain, hurt and frustration in our homes. We will be able to laugh more often. Friends, relatives and well-wishers, please help us to instill good habits in our children. Teach them cooperation, love, and concern for others. This will foster joy for all.

Printed in the United States
By Bookmasters